Clifford's BIG Learning Treasury

Clifford's Manners
Clifford's ABC
Clifford's Word Book
Count on Clifford

Norman Bridwell

Children's Book-of-the-Month Club
New York

Clifford's
MANNERS

Dedicated to Robbie and Alex

I'm Emily Elizabeth,
and this is Clifford.

Everyone loves Clifford
because he has good manners.
I taught him myself.

Clifford says "please" when he asks for something.

Say please.

Say thank you.

He says "thank you" when he gets something.

And he writes a thank-you note
when someone gives him a present.

**Send
thank-you
notes.**

Wait your turn.

Clifford loves to go to the movies.
He waits his turn in line.

If Clifford has a snack,
he puts the empty bag into the litter basket.
Clifford hates litterbugs.

Don't litter.

Say excuse
me.

Clifford says "excuse me" when he needs
to pass in front of people.

He never talks during the show.
Talking disturbs others.

**Do not talk
during a show.**

Sh-h-h!

Use your handkerchief.

KERTY-SHOO

When Clifford has to sneeze,
he uses a handkerchief or tissue.
It's a good thing he does.

Clifford has many friends.
He shares his toys with them.

Share.

**Put your
toys away.**

Clifford puts his toys away when he is through.
His friends help. They have good manners,

Clifford is a terrific tennis player.
He obeys all the rules of the game.

Follow the
rules.

Talk—
don't hit.

Sometimes players disagree.
When Clifford is angry, he does not hit.
He just says what he feels.

Clifford is a good sport.
He smiles when he loses.
And he does not boast when he wins.

Be a good
sport.

Call ahead.

Clifford loves to go visiting.
When he visits his sister in the country,
he always calls ahead.

Clifford always arrives on time.

Don't be late.

Knock before
you walk in.

He knocks on the door before he enters.

He wipes his feet first.

Wipe your feet.

Clifford kisses his sister.
He shakes hands with her friend.

Shake hands.

Wash up
before
you eat.

Clifford's sister has dinner ready.
Clifford washes his hands before he eats.

Clifford chews his food with his mouth closed.
He never talks with his mouth full.

Don't talk with your mouth full.

Clifford helps with the clean-up.

Help
clean up.

Say
good-bye.

Then he says "thank you" and "good-bye"
to his sister and to his friend.

Everyone loves Clifford's manners.
That's why everyone loves Clifford!

Have good manners.

scarecrow

elephant

dog

elf

Clifford's
ABC

alligator

beaver

cow

Aa

Aa
accordion
acorns
alligator
anchor
ant
anvil
armadillo
axe

accordion

axe

armadillo

anvil

acorns

alligat[or]

ant

anchor

Bb

bird

ball

bat

boots

basket

balloon

boy

boat

butterfly

beaver

bottle

baby

Bb
baby
ball
balloon
basket
bat
beaver
bird
boat
boots
bottle
boy
butterfly

Cc

Cc
cactus
cake
candle
cape
cat
checks
clown
collar
cook
cow

collar

cow

cat

cook

candle

cake

cactus

cape

clown

checks

Dd

dragon

dolphin

dog

mmy

drum

derby

dandelion

Dd
dandelion
derby
dog
dolphin
dragon
drum
dummy

eagle

egg

earring

elephant

eel

Eskimo

elf

Ee

Ee
eagle
earring
eel
egg
elephant
elf
Eskimo

Ff

frog

fly

fish

flag

fire

fairy

flea

funnel

fox

flower

Ff
fairy
fire
fish
flag
flea
flower
fly
fox
frog
funnel

ghost

gorilla

giraffe

Gg

garden

goat

Gg
garbage can
garden
ghost
giraffe
glove
goat
gorilla

glove

garbage c

Hh

helicopter

harp

house

horse

hollyhock

hummingbird

hat

horn

tack

hippopotamus

Hh
harp
hat
haystack
helicopter
hippopotamus
hollyhock
horn
horse
house
hummingbird

Ii

Ii
ice cream cone
igloo
iguana
ink
iris
iron

iguana

igloo

iris

ink

iron

ice cr

Jj

jet

juggler

jogger

jack-o'-lantern

jester

jacks

Jj
jack-o'-lantern
jacks
jester
jet
jogger
juggler

Kk Ll

Kk
kangaroo
karate
kayak
kitten
knight
knitting
koala

Ll
lamb
lasso
leopard
lily
lion
lobster
log
lumberjack

koala

knight

lobster

lily

lasso

karate

lumberj[ack]

knitting

kitten

log

kangaroo

leopard

lamb

lion

kayak

Mm

moon

mop

map

mask

monkey

mittens

mouse

magician

marionette

magnet

Mm
magician
magnet
map
marionette
mask
mittens
monkey
moon
mop
mouse

note

nest

nun

nutcracker

nut

noodles

nurse

ne

Nn
nest
net
noodles
note
nun
nurse
nut
nutcracker

Oo

owl

orchid

ostrich

orange

octopus

overalls

oar

Oo
oar
octopus
orange
orchid
ostrich
overalls
owl

P

parachute

P p

palm

pineapple

pan[da]

picture

pirate

pear

paintb[rush]

pony

palet[te]

pig

porcupine

Pp
paintbrush
palette
palm
panda
parachute
pear
picture
pig
pineapple
pirate
pony
porcupine

Qq

Qq
quail
quartet
queen
question
quilt

quail

quartet

question

queen

quilt

Rr

rain

rhinoceros

rainbow

rocket

robot

rope

racket

rug

raccoon

rabbit

rake

roller skate

radishes

Rr
rabbit
raccoon
racket
radishes
rain
rainbow
rake
rhinoceros
robot
rocket
roller skate
rope
rug

Ss

Saturn

star

scarecrow

sleep

saxophone

soccer ball

sausage

sandwich

seesaw

squirrel

snail

seal

stool

Ss
sandwich
Saturn
sausage
saxophone
scarecrow
seal
seesaw
sleep
snail
soccer ball
squirrel
star
stool

Tt

Tt
table
teapot
teddy bear
telescope
television
tent
tepee
tiger
tractor
train
turtle

tent

tepee

tractor

tiger

telescope

televi...

teapot

train

teddy bear

turtle

table

Uu

umbrella

UFO

unicorn

umpire

urn

ukulele

unicycle

Uu
UFO
ukulele
umbrella
umpire
unicorn
unicycle
urn

Vv

Vv
vacuum cleaner
valentine
vampire
vase
violets
violin
vise
volcano

volcano

vampire

valentine

vio

violin

vise

vacuum cleaner

vase

Ww

whale

waves

walrus

wrenches

wheelbarrow

witch

wolf

worm

waffles

wagon

Ww
waffles
wagon
walrus
waves
whale
wheelbarrow
witch
wolf
worm
wrenches

W

Xx Yy

Xx
x-ray
xylophone

Yy
yacht
yak
yarn
yawn
yo-yo

xylophone

yacht

x-ray

yak

yawn

yarn

yo-yo

zeppelin

ZOO

zebra

zipper

zither

Zz

Zz
zebra
zeppelin
zipper
zither
zoo

z

Clifford's
WORD BOOK

Dedicated to Nadia Miret.
— N.B.

sky

tree

house

girl

dog

grass

My name is Emily Elizabeth
and this is my big red dog, Clifford.

picture

plant

Clifford is too big to fit inside my room.
But he can still keep me company.

hook

clock

bed

book

dresser

pillow

blanket

slippers

hanger

rug

radio

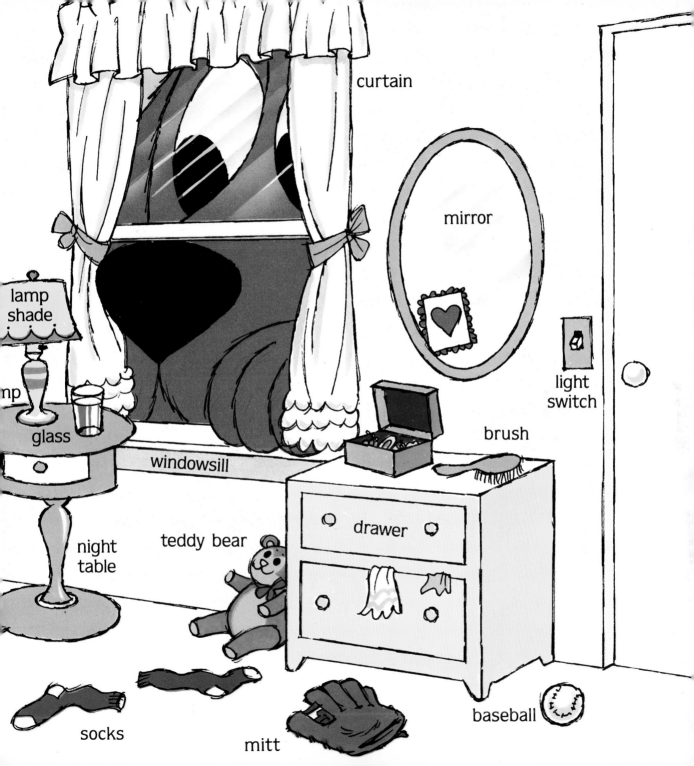

curtain

mirror

lamp
shade

light
switch

np

glass

brush

windowsill

drawer

night
table

teddy bear

socks

mitt

baseball

Like all dogs, Clifford has a favorite toy.
What's your favorite toy?

kite

football

glider

yo-yo

jump rope

rocking horse

wagon

train

toy car

soccer ball

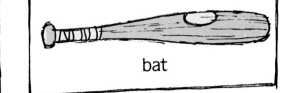

bat

stuffed monkey

dinosaur

crayons

tennis racket

puzzle

dollhouse

carriage

baseball

tea set

blocks

top

rattle

jacks

doll

flag

streetlight

BARBER SHOP

barber pole

49

bananas

watermelons

pineapples

bench

fire hydrant

And he likes to go for walks.
This is the main street of our town.

FRUITS AND VEGETABLES

HARDWARE

CLOTHING

13

saw

rake

pliers

shovel

paint

hammer

drill

jeans

blouse

dress

shorts

socks

shoes

waste basket

sidewalk

mailbox

celery

traffic light

letter

manhole cover

Everybody knows Clifford.
And everybody likes Clifford.

photographer

magician

baseball player

carpenter

chef

farmer

jester

fire fighter

uto mechanic

musician

jockey

fisherman

Clifford waits for me while I'm in school.
I can see him outside the window.

bulletin board

poster

lunch box

aquarium

crossing guard

calendar

scarf

chair

ruler

train

truck

unicycle

tugboat

jet

car

jeep

helicopter

hot-air balloon

race car

sailboat

Clifford likes things that move.
I tell him not to chase cars.
But sometimes he forgets.

motorcycle

canoe

basketball hoop

basketball

ice-cream vendor

birdbath

jogger

skateboard

pogo stick

In the afternoon, we play in the park.
Clifford is even more fun than a swing!

swings

jungle gym

fountain

picnic table

slide

sandbox

seesaw

guitar

trumpet

xylophone

tambourine

bow

violin

triangle

piano

saxophone

Clifford loves listening to music.
He is a good singer.

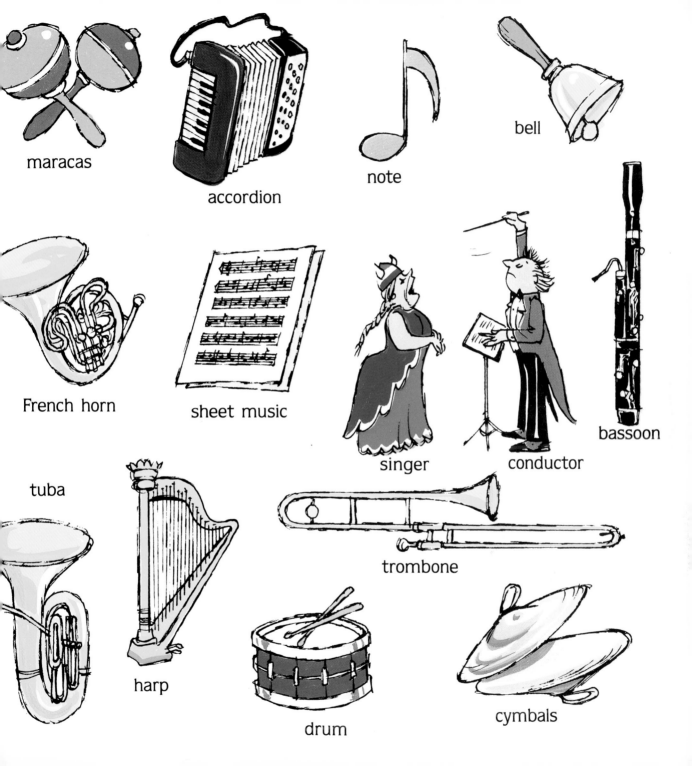

maracas

accordion

note

bell

French horn

sheet music

singer

conductor

bassoon

tuba

harp

trombone

drum

cymbals

apple trees

field

scarecro[w]

sheep

sunflowers

clothes line

farmhouse

water pump

basket

wheelbarro[w]

birdbath

porch

chickens

Clifford visits a farm.

igloo

beehive

grass hut

nest

tepee

camper

dog house

CLIFFORD

castle

tent

house

Clifford lives in a dog house,
a very big dog house.

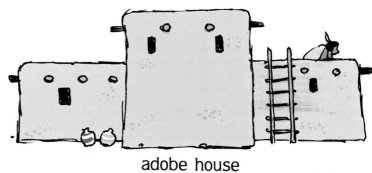

adobe house

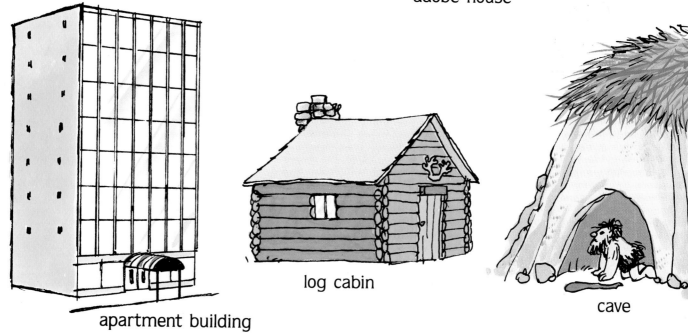

apartment building

log cabin

cave

trapeze

Once the circus came to town.
Clifford helped to put on a show.

pie

hoop

ringmaster

tiger

juggler

balancing pole

tightrope walker

tent pole

audience

bareback rider

elephant

horse

clowns

dogs

clown car

sea lion

turtle

camel

kangaroo

Clifford is bigger than an elephant!

rhinoceros

penguin

octopus

panda

gorilla

deer

In the summer we go to the beach.
Clifford does the dog paddle.

umbrella

lighthouse

ball

dog

surfboard

towel

chair

bag

straw hat

picnic basket

sandwich

seagull

sunglasses

blanke

sun

seaplane

ocean

raft

lobster

sandpipers

seaweed

sand

horseshoe crab

shovel

starfish

sand castle

WHITE

snowman

dove

shirt

BLACK

ants

bat

bow tie

RED

Clifford

apple

heart

ORANGE

pumpkin

carrots

oranges

YELLOW

lemon

daffodil

cheese

Clifford's favorite color is red.

GREEN

leaf

peas

grasshopper

BLUE

blueberries

ribbon

cap

PURPLE

violets

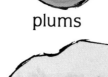
plums

crocuses

GRAY

mouse

stone

slacks

PINK

cupcake

rose

strawberry ice cream

BROWN

acorns

pinecone

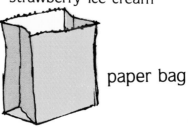
paper bag

Today is a special day!

HAPPY BIRTHDAY, CLIFFORD!

banner

party hat

noisemaker

plate

candles

bowl

cups

cake

ice-cream scoop

ice cream

presen

balloon

tablecloth

bone

table

For Timothy, Brian, and Julie Stanton

COUNT ON
Clifford

Count **one** Clifford.

one

Hi! My name is Emily Elizabeth.

This is my dog, Clifford. There is only **one** Clifford in all the world.

On Clifford's birthday, I gave him a party.

one

Count **one** Clifford.

two

We were going to have a lot of balloons.
I blew up **two** balloons. Then I got tired.

Clifford tried to blow up the rest. Clifford blew a little too hard, so we just had **two** balloons.

Count
two balloons.
Count **two** girls.
Count **two** boys.

two

three

Count **three** presents.

I bought Clifford **three** presents. I wrapped them up. I was going to put bows on them.

But Clifford found the ribbons first.
What a mess!

Count
three windows.

three

four

Count
four party hats.

I invited Clifford's dog friends.
Four of them came.
I didn't ask any cats.

Count **four** of Clifford's dog friends.

Count **four** houses.

four

five

Count **five** chairs.
Count **two**
yellow chairs.

We played musical chairs.
I set up **five** chairs.

We ran around and around.
When the music stopped,
Clifford was the first
to sit down. No more
musical chairs.

five

six

Count **six** trees.

We played Hide-and-Seek. Clifford hid behind **six** trees.

6

We found Clifford anyway.

six

seven

Count
seven candles.
Count
seven forks.

Then it was time fo
Clifford's cake. I pu
seven candles on th
cake.

HAPPY BIRTHDAY CLIFFORD

7

Clifford blew out the candles.
We had ice cream instead.

seven

eight

Clifford opened his gifts.
Everyone had the same idea.

Clifford got **eight** sacks of dog food.

Count
four red sacks.
Count **four**
yellow sacks.
Count all
eight sacks.

eight

Count
four red balls.
Count **five**
yellow balls.
Count all
nine balls.

nine

We had a clown at the party.
The clown juggled **nine** balls.

Clifford wanted to juggle, too.
Oops!

nine

ten

Count **three** gray cats.

Count **three** white cats.

Count **four** striped cats.

Count all **ten** cats.

Then some cats came. They wanted to play games, too. We asked them to join us. They did. **One, two, three, four, five, six, seven, eight, nine, ten.**

Ten cats in all!

ten

We were having fun.
Then I felt a raindrop.

Count the
children.
Count the dogs.
Don't forget to
count Clifford.

Oh, no! It was raining.
The party would be ruined.

Count the boys.
Count the girls.

But Clifford knew what to do. He saved the party. I always knew I could count on Clifford.